PASSWORD ORGANIZER

Internet, Email and Phone Passwords

Wi-Fi Network Name:	
Wi-Fi Password:	

Email Address:	
Password:	

Email Address 2:	
Password:	

Phone Number:	
PIN Code:	
PUK Code:	

Phone Number 2:	
PIN Code:	
PUK Code:	

Website:	
Username:	
Password:	
Notes / Security Questions:	

Website:	
Username:	
Password:	
Notes / Security Questions:	

Website:	
Username:	
Password:	
Notes / Security Questions:	

Website:	
Username:	
Password:	
Notes / Security Questions:	

A

Website:	
Username:	
Password:	
Notes / Security Questions:	

Website:	
Username:	
Password:	
Notes / Security Questions:	

Website:	
Username:	
Password:	
Notes / Security Questions:	

Website:	
Username:	
Password:	
Notes / Security Questions:	

Website:	
Username:	
Password:	
Notes / Security Questions:	

Website:	
Username:	
Password:	
Notes / Security Questions:	

Website:	
Username:	
Password:	
Notes / Security Questions:	

Website:	
Username:	
Password:	
Notes / Security Questions:	

Website:	
Username:	
Password:	
Notes / Security Questions:	

Website:	
Username:	
Password:	
Notes / Security Questions:	

Website:	
Username:	
Password:	
Notes / Security Questions:	

Website:	
Username:	
Password:	
Notes / Security Questions:	

Website:	
Username:	
Password:	
Notes / Security Questions:	

Website:	
Username:	
Password:	
Notes / Security Questions:	

Website:	
Username:	
Password:	
Notes / Security Questions:	

Website:	
Username:	
Password:	
Notes / Security Questions:	

Website:	
Username:	
Password:	
Notes / Security Questions:	

Website:	
Username:	
Password:	
Notes / Security Questions:	

Website:	
Username:	
Password:	
Notes / Security Questions:	

Website:	
Username:	
Password:	
Notes / Security Questions:	

Website:	
Username:	
Password:	
Notes / Security Questions:	

Website:	
Username:	
Password:	
Notes / Security Questions:	

Website:	
Username:	
Password:	
Notes / Security Questions:	

Website:	
Username:	
Password:	
Notes / Security Questions:	

Website:	
Username:	
Password:	
Notes / Security Questions:	

Website:	
Username:	
Password:	
Notes / Security Questions:	

Website:	
Username:	
Password:	
Notes / Security Questions:	

Website:	
Username:	
Password:	
Notes / Security Questions:	

Website:	
Username:	
Password:	
Notes / Security Questions:	

Website:	
Username:	
Password:	
Notes / Security Questions:	

Website:	
Username:	
Password:	
Notes / Security Questions:	

Website:	
Username:	
Password:	
Notes / Security Questions:	

Website:	
Username:	
Password:	
Notes / Security Questions:	

Website:	
Username:	
Password:	
Notes / Security Questions:	

Website:	
Username:	
Password:	
Notes / Security Questions:	

Website:	
Username:	
Password:	
Notes / Security Questions:	

C

Website:	
Username:	
Password:	
Notes / Security Questions:	

Website:	
Username:	
Password:	
Notes / Security Questions:	

Website:	
Username:	
Password:	
Notes / Security Questions:	

Website:	
Username:	
Password:	
Notes / Security Questions:	

Website:	
Username:	
Password:	
Notes / Security Questions:	

Website:	
Username:	
Password:	
Notes / Security Questions:	

Website:	
Username:	
Password:	
Notes / Security Questions:	

Website:	
Username:	
Password:	
Notes / Security Questions:	

Website:	
Username:	
Password:	
Notes / Security Questions:	

Website:	
Username:	
Password:	
Notes / Security Questions:	

Website:	
Username:	
Password:	
Notes / Security Questions:	

Website:	
Username:	
Password:	
Notes / Security Questions:	

Website:	
Username:	
Password:	
Notes / Security Questions:	

Website:	
Username:	
Password:	
Notes / Security Questions:	

Website:	
Username:	
Password:	
Notes / Security Questions:	

Website:	
Username:	
Password:	
Notes / Security Questions:	

Website:	
Username:	
Password:	
Notes / Security Questions:	

Website:	
Username:	
Password:	
Notes / Security Questions:	

Website:	
Username:	
Password:	
Notes / Security Questions:	

Website:	
Username:	
Password:	
Notes / Security Questions:	

Website:	
Username:	
Password:	
Notes / Security Questions:	

Website:	
Username:	
Password:	
Notes / Security Questions:	

Website:	
Username:	
Password:	
Notes / Security Questions:	

Website:	
Username:	
Password:	
Notes / Security Questions:	

E

Website:	
Username:	
Password:	
Notes / Security Questions:	

Website:	
Username:	
Password:	
Notes / Security Questions:	

Website:	
Username:	
Password:	
Notes / Security Questions:	

Website:	
Username:	
Password:	
Notes / Security Questions:	

Website:	
Username:	
Password:	
Notes / Security Questions:	

Website:	
Username:	
Password:	
Notes / Security Questions:	

Website:	
Username:	
Password:	
Notes / Security Questions:	

Website:	
Username:	
Password:	
Notes / Security Questions:	

E

Website:	
Username:	
Password:	
Notes / Security Questions:	

Website:	
Username:	
Password:	
Notes / Security Questions:	

Website:	
Username:	
Password:	
Notes / Security Questions:	

Website:	
Username:	
Password:	
Notes / Security Questions:	

E

Website:	
Username:	
Password:	
Notes / Security Questions:	

Website:	
Username:	
Password:	
Notes / Security Questions:	

Website:	
Username:	
Password:	
Notes / Security Questions:	

Website:	
Username:	
Password:	
Notes / Security Questions:	

Website:	
Username:	
Password:	
Notes / Security Questions:	

Website:	
Username:	
Password:	
Notes / Security Questions:	

Website:	
Username:	
Password:	
Notes / Security Questions:	

Website:	
Username:	
Password:	
Notes / Security Questions:	

Website:	
Username:	
Password:	
Notes / Security Questions:	

Website:	
Username:	
Password:	
Notes / Security Questions:	

Website:	
Username:	
Password:	
Notes / Security Questions:	

Website:	
Username:	
Password:	
Notes / Security Questions:	

Website:	
Username:	
Password:	
Notes / Security Questions:	

Website:	
Username:	
Password:	
Notes / Security Questions:	

Website:	
Username:	
Password:	
Notes / Security Questions:	

Website:	
Username:	
Password:	
Notes / Security Questions:	

Website:	
Username:	
Password:	
Notes / Security Questions:	

Website:	
Username:	
Password:	
Notes / Security Questions:	

Website:	
Username:	
Password:	
Notes / Security Questions:	

Website:	
Username:	
Password:	
Notes / Security Questions:	

Website:	
Username:	
Password:	
Notes / Security Questions:	

Website:	
Username:	
Password:	
Notes / Security Questions:	

Website:	
Username:	
Password:	
Notes / Security Questions:	

Website:	
Username:	
Password:	
Notes / Security Questions:	

Website:	
Username:	
Password:	
Notes / Security Questions:	

Website:	
Username:	
Password:	
Notes / Security Questions:	

Website:	
Username:	
Password:	
Notes / Security Questions:	

Website:	
Username:	
Password:	
Notes / Security Questions:	

Website:	
Username:	
Password:	
Notes / Security Questions:	

Website:	
Username:	
Password:	
Notes / Security Questions:	

Website:	
Username:	
Password:	
Notes / Security Questions:	

Website:	
Username:	
Password:	
Notes / Security Questions:	

Website:	
Username:	
Password:	
Notes / Security Questions:	

Website:	
Username:	
Password:	
Notes / Security Questions:	

Website:	
Username:	
Password:	
Notes / Security Questions:	

Website:	
Username:	
Password:	
Notes / Security Questions:	

Website:	
Username:	
Password:	
Notes / Security Questions:	

Website:	
Username:	
Password:	
Notes / Security Questions:	

Website:	
Username:	
Password:	
Notes / Security Questions:	

Website:	
Username:	
Password:	
Notes / Security Questions:	

Website:	
Username:	
Password:	
Notes / Security Questions:	

Website:	
Username:	
Password:	
Notes / Security Questions:	

Website:	
Username:	
Password:	
Notes / Security Questions:	

Website:	
Username:	
Password:	
Notes / Security Questions:	

H

Website:	
Username:	
Password:	
Notes / Security Questions:	

Website:	
Username:	
Password:	
Notes / Security Questions:	

Website:	
Username:	
Password:	
Notes / Security Questions:	

Website:	
Username:	
Password:	
Notes / Security Questions:	

Website:	
Username:	
Password:	
Notes / Security Questions:	

Website:	
Username:	
Password:	
Notes / Security Questions:	

Website:	
Username:	
Password:	
Notes / Security Questions:	

Website:	
Username:	
Password:	
Notes / Security Questions:	

Website:	
Username:	
Password:	
Notes / Security Questions:	

Website:	
Username:	
Password:	
Notes / Security Questions:	

Website:	
Username:	
Password:	
Notes / Security Questions:	

Website:	
Username:	
Password:	
Notes / Security Questions:	

Website:	
Username:	
Password:	
Notes / Security Questions:	

Website:	
Username:	
Password:	
Notes / Security Questions:	

Website:	
Username:	
Password:	
Notes / Security Questions:	

Website:	
Username:	
Password:	
Notes / Security Questions:	

Website:	
Username:	
Password:	
Notes / Security Questions:	

Website:	
Username:	
Password:	
Notes / Security Questions:	

Website:	
Username:	
Password:	
Notes / Security Questions:	

Website:	
Username:	
Password:	
Notes / Security Questions:	

Website:	
Username:	
Password:	
Notes / Security Questions:	

Website:	
Username:	
Password:	
Notes / Security Questions:	

Website:	
Username:	
Password:	
Notes / Security Questions:	

Website:	
Username:	
Password:	
Notes / Security Questions:	

Website:	
Username:	
Password:	
Notes / Security Questions:	

Website:	
Username:	
Password:	
Notes / Security Questions:	

Website:	
Username:	
Password:	
Notes / Security Questions:	

Website:	
Username:	
Password:	
Notes / Security Questions:	

J

Website:	
Username:	
Password:	
Notes / Security Questions:	

Website:	
Username:	
Password:	
Notes / Security Questions:	

Website:	
Username:	
Password:	
Notes / Security Questions:	

Website:	
Username:	
Password:	
Notes / Security Questions:	

J

Website:	
Username:	
Password:	
Notes / Security Questions:	

Website:	
Username:	
Password:	
Notes / Security Questions:	

Website:	
Username:	
Password:	
Notes / Security Questions:	

Website:	
Username:	
Password:	
Notes / Security Questions:	

J

Website:	
Username:	
Password:	
Notes / Security Questions:	

Website:	
Username:	
Password:	
Notes / Security Questions:	

Website:	
Username:	
Password:	
Notes / Security Questions:	

Website:	
Username:	
Password:	
Notes / Security Questions:	

Website:	
Username:	
Password:	
Notes / Security Questions:	

Website:	
Username:	
Password:	
Notes / Security Questions:	

Website:	
Username:	
Password:	
Notes / Security Questions:	

Website:	
Username:	
Password:	
Notes / Security Questions:	

Website:	
Username:	
Password:	
Notes / Security Questions:	

Website:	
Username:	
Password:	
Notes / Security Questions:	

Website:	
Username:	
Password:	
Notes / Security Questions:	

Website:	
Username:	
Password:	
Notes / Security Questions:	

Website:	
Username:	
Password:	
Notes / Security Questions:	

Website:	
Username:	
Password:	
Notes / Security Questions:	

Website:	
Username:	
Password:	
Notes / Security Questions:	

Website:	
Username:	
Password:	
Notes / Security Questions:	

Website:	
Username:	
Password:	
Notes / Security Questions:	

Website:	
Username:	
Password:	
Notes / Security Questions:	

Website:	
Username:	
Password:	
Notes / Security Questions:	

Website:	
Username:	
Password:	
Notes / Security Questions:	

L

Website:	
Username:	
Password:	
Notes / Security Questions:	

Website:	
Username:	
Password:	
Notes / Security Questions:	

Website:	
Username:	
Password:	
Notes / Security Questions:	

Website:	
Username:	
Password:	
Notes / Security Questions:	

L

Website:	
Username:	
Password:	
Notes / Security Questions:	

Website:	
Username:	
Password:	
Notes / Security Questions:	

Website:	
Username:	
Password:	
Notes / Security Questions:	

Website:	
Username:	
Password:	
Notes / Security Questions:	

L

Website:	
Username:	
Password:	
Notes / Security Questions:	

Website:	
Username:	
Password:	
Notes / Security Questions:	

Website:	
Username:	
Password:	
Notes / Security Questions:	

Website:	
Username:	
Password:	
Notes / Security Questions:	

Website:	
Username:	
Password:	
Notes / Security Questions:	

Website:	
Username:	
Password:	
Notes / Security Questions:	

Website:	
Username:	
Password:	
Notes / Security Questions:	

Website:	
Username:	
Password:	
Notes / Security Questions:	

Website:	
Username:	
Password:	
Notes / Security Questions:	

Website:	
Username:	
Password:	
Notes / Security Questions:	

Website:	
Username:	
Password:	
Notes / Security Questions:	

Website:	
Username:	
Password:	
Notes / Security Questions:	

Website:	
Username:	
Password:	
Notes / Security Questions:	

Website:	
Username:	
Password:	
Notes / Security Questions:	

Website:	
Username:	
Password:	
Notes / Security Questions:	

Website:	
Username:	
Password:	
Notes / Security Questions:	

Website:	
Username:	
Password:	
Notes / Security Questions:	

Website:	
Username:	
Password:	
Notes / Security Questions:	

Website:	
Username:	
Password:	
Notes / Security Questions:	

Website:	
Username:	
Password:	
Notes / Security Questions:	

Website:	
Username:	
Password:	
Notes / Security Questions:	

Website:	
Username:	
Password:	
Notes / Security Questions:	

Website:	
Username:	
Password:	
Notes / Security Questions:	

Website:	
Username:	
Password:	
Notes / Security Questions:	

Website:	
Username:	
Password:	
Notes / Security Questions:	

Website:	
Username:	
Password:	
Notes / Security Questions:	

Website:	
Username:	
Password:	
Notes / Security Questions:	

Website:	
Username:	
Password:	
Notes / Security Questions:	

Website:	
Username:	
Password:	
Notes / Security Questions:	

Website:	
Username:	
Password:	
Notes / Security Questions:	

Website:	
Username:	
Password:	
Notes / Security Questions:	

Website:	
Username:	
Password:	
Notes / Security Questions:	

Website:	
Username:	
Password:	
Notes / Security Questions:	

Website:	
Username:	
Password:	
Notes / Security Questions:	

Website:	
Username:	
Password:	
Notes / Security Questions:	

Website:	
Username:	
Password:	
Notes / Security Questions:	

Website:	
Username:	
Password:	
Notes / Security Questions:	

Website:	
Username:	
Password:	
Notes / Security Questions:	

Website:	
Username:	
Password:	
Notes / Security Questions:	

Website:	
Username:	
Password:	
Notes / Security Questions:	

O

Website:	
Username:	
Password:	
Notes / Security Questions:	

Website:	
Username:	
Password:	
Notes / Security Questions:	

Website:	
Username:	
Password:	
Notes / Security Questions:	

Website:	
Username:	
Password:	
Notes / Security Questions:	

Website:	
Username:	
Password:	
Notes / Security Questions:	

Website:	
Username:	
Password:	
Notes / Security Questions:	

Website:	
Username:	
Password:	
Notes / Security Questions:	

Website:	
Username:	
Password:	
Notes / Security Questions:	

O

Website:	
Username:	
Password:	
Notes / Security Questions:	

Website:	
Username:	
Password:	
Notes / Security Questions:	

Website:	
Username:	
Password:	
Notes / Security Questions:	

Website:	
Username:	
Password:	
Notes / Security Questions:	

Website:	
Username:	
Password:	
Notes / Security Questions:	

Website:	
Username:	
Password:	
Notes / Security Questions:	

Website:	
Username:	
Password:	
Notes / Security Questions:	

Website:	
Username:	
Password:	
Notes / Security Questions:	

Website:	
Username:	
Password:	
Notes / Security Questions:	

Website:	
Username:	
Password:	
Notes / Security Questions:	

Website:	
Username:	
Password:	
Notes / Security Questions:	

Website:	
Username:	
Password:	
Notes / Security Questions:	

Website:	
Username:	
Password:	
Notes / Security Questions:	

Website:	
Username:	
Password:	
Notes / Security Questions:	

Website:	
Username:	
Password:	
Notes / Security Questions:	

Website:	
Username:	
Password:	
Notes / Security Questions:	

Website:	
Username:	
Password:	
Notes / Security Questions:	

Website:	
Username:	
Password:	
Notes / Security Questions:	

Website:	
Username:	
Password:	
Notes / Security Questions:	

Website:	
Username:	
Password:	
Notes / Security Questions:	

Website:	
Username:	
Password:	
Notes / Security Questions:	

Website:	
Username:	
Password:	
Notes / Security Questions:	

Website:	
Username:	
Password:	
Notes / Security Questions:	

Website:	
Username:	
Password:	
Notes / Security Questions:	

Q

Website:	
Username:	
Password:	
Notes / Security Questions:	

Website:	
Username:	
Password:	
Notes / Security Questions:	

Website:	
Username:	
Password:	
Notes / Security Questions:	

Website:	
Username:	
Password:	
Notes / Security Questions:	

Website:	
Username:	
Password:	
Notes / Security Questions:	

Website:	
Username:	
Password:	
Notes / Security Questions:	

Website:	
Username:	
Password:	
Notes / Security Questions:	

Website:	
Username:	
Password:	
Notes / Security Questions:	

Q

Website:	
Username:	
Password:	
Notes / Security Questions:	

Website:	
Username:	
Password:	
Notes / Security Questions:	

Website:	
Username:	
Password:	
Notes / Security Questions:	

Website:	
Username:	
Password:	
Notes / Security Questions:	

Q

Website:	
Username:	
Password:	
Notes / Security Questions:	

Website:	
Username:	
Password:	
Notes / Security Questions:	

Website:	
Username:	
Password:	
Notes / Security Questions:	

Website:	
Username:	
Password:	
Notes / Security Questions:	

Website:	
Username:	
Password:	
Notes / Security Questions:	

Website:	
Username:	
Password:	
Notes / Security Questions:	

Website:	
Username:	
Password:	
Notes / Security Questions:	

Website:	
Username:	
Password:	
Notes / Security Questions:	

Website:	
Username:	
Password:	
Notes / Security Questions:	

Website:	
Username:	
Password:	
Notes / Security Questions:	

Website:	
Username:	
Password:	
Notes / Security Questions:	

Website:	
Username:	
Password:	
Notes / Security Questions:	

Website:	
Username:	
Password:	
Notes / Security Questions:	

Website:	
Username:	
Password:	
Notes / Security Questions:	

Website:	
Username:	
Password:	
Notes / Security Questions:	

Website:	
Username:	
Password:	
Notes / Security Questions:	

Website:	
Username:	
Password:	
Notes / Security Questions:	

Website:	
Username:	
Password:	
Notes / Security Questions:	

Website:	
Username:	
Password:	
Notes / Security Questions:	

Website:	
Username:	
Password:	
Notes / Security Questions:	

Website:	
Username:	
Password:	
Notes / Security Questions:	

Website:	
Username:	
Password:	
Notes / Security Questions:	

Website:	
Username:	
Password:	
Notes / Security Questions:	

Website:	
Username:	
Password:	
Notes / Security Questions:	

S

Website:	
Username:	
Password:	
Notes / Security Questions:	

Website:	
Username:	
Password:	
Notes / Security Questions:	

Website:	
Username:	
Password:	
Notes / Security Questions:	

Website:	
Username:	
Password:	
Notes / Security Questions:	

S

Website:	
Username:	
Password:	
Notes / Security Questions:	

Website:	
Username:	
Password:	
Notes / Security Questions:	

Website:	
Username:	
Password:	
Notes / Security Questions:	

Website:	
Username:	
Password:	
Notes / Security Questions:	

S

Website:	
Username:	
Password:	
Notes / Security Questions:	

Website:	
Username:	
Password:	
Notes / Security Questions:	

Website:	
Username:	
Password:	
Notes / Security Questions:	

Website:	
Username:	
Password:	
Notes / Security Questions:	

Website:	
Username:	
Password:	
Notes / Security Questions:	

Website:	
Username:	
Password:	
Notes / Security Questions:	

Website:	
Username:	
Password:	
Notes / Security Questions:	

Website:	
Username:	
Password:	
Notes / Security Questions:	

Website:	
Username:	
Password:	
Notes / Security Questions:	

Website:	
Username:	
Password:	
Notes / Security Questions:	

Website:	
Username:	
Password:	
Notes / Security Questions:	

Website:	
Username:	
Password:	
Notes / Security Questions:	

Website:	
Username:	
Password:	
Notes / Security Questions:	

Website:	
Username:	
Password:	
Notes / Security Questions:	

Website:	
Username:	
Password:	
Notes / Security Questions:	

Website:	
Username:	
Password:	
Notes / Security Questions:	

Website:	
Username:	
Password:	
Notes / Security Questions:	

Website:	
Username:	
Password:	
Notes / Security Questions:	

Website:	
Username:	
Password:	
Notes / Security Questions:	

Website:	
Username:	
Password:	
Notes / Security Questions:	

Website:	
Username:	
Password:	
Notes / Security Questions:	

Website:	
Username:	
Password:	
Notes / Security Questions:	

Website:	
Username:	
Password:	
Notes / Security Questions:	

Website:	
Username:	
Password:	
Notes / Security Questions:	

Website:	
Username:	
Password:	
Notes / Security Questions:	

Website:	
Username:	
Password:	
Notes / Security Questions:	

Website:	
Username:	
Password:	
Notes / Security Questions:	

Website:	
Username:	
Password:	
Notes / Security Questions:	

Website:	
Username:	
Password:	
Notes / Security Questions:	

Website:	
Username:	
Password:	
Notes / Security Questions:	

Website:	
Username:	
Password:	
Notes / Security Questions:	

Website:	
Username:	
Password:	
Notes / Security Questions:	

Website:	
Username:	
Password:	
Notes / Security Questions:	

Website:	
Username:	
Password:	
Notes / Security Questions:	

Website:	
Username:	
Password:	
Notes / Security Questions:	

Website:	
Username:	
Password:	
Notes / Security Questions:	

Website:	
Username:	
Password:	
Notes / Security Questions:	

Website:	
Username:	
Password:	
Notes / Security Questions:	

Website:	
Username:	
Password:	
Notes / Security Questions:	

Website:	
Username:	
Password:	
Notes / Security Questions:	

Website:	
Username:	
Password:	
Notes / Security Questions:	

Website:	
Username:	
Password:	
Notes / Security Questions:	

Website:	
Username:	
Password:	
Notes / Security Questions:	

Website:	
Username:	
Password:	
Notes / Security Questions:	

Website:	
Username:	
Password:	
Notes / Security Questions:	

Website:	
Username:	
Password:	
Notes / Security Questions:	

Website:	
Username:	
Password:	
Notes / Security Questions:	

Website:	
Username:	
Password:	
Notes / Security Questions:	

Website:	
Username:	
Password:	
Notes / Security Questions:	

Website:	
Username:	
Password:	
Notes / Security Questions:	

Website:	
Username:	
Password:	
Notes / Security Questions:	

Website:	
Username:	
Password:	
Notes / Security Questions:	

Website:	
Username:	
Password:	
Notes / Security Questions:	

Website:	
Username:	
Password:	
Notes / Security Questions:	

Website:	
Username:	
Password:	
Notes / Security Questions:	

Website:	
Username:	
Password:	
Notes / Security Questions:	

Website:	
Username:	
Password:	
Notes / Security Questions:	

Website:	
Username:	
Password:	
Notes / Security Questions:	

Website:	
Username:	
Password:	
Notes / Security Questions:	

Website:	
Username:	
Password:	
Notes / Security Questions:	

Website:	
Username:	
Password:	
Notes / Security Questions:	

Website:	
Username:	
Password:	
Notes / Security Questions:	

Website:	
Username:	
Password:	
Notes / Security Questions:	

Website:	
Username:	
Password:	
Notes / Security Questions:	

Website:	
Username:	
Password:	
Notes / Security Questions:	

Website:	
Username:	
Password:	
Notes / Security Questions:	

Website:	
Username:	
Password:	
Notes / Security Questions:	

Website:	
Username:	
Password:	
Notes / Security Questions:	

Website:	
Username:	
Password:	
Notes / Security Questions:	

Website:	
Username:	
Password:	
Notes / Security Questions:	

Website:	
Username:	
Password:	
Notes / Security Questions:	

Website:	
Username:	
Password:	
Notes / Security Questions:	

Website:	
Username:	
Password:	
Notes / Security Questions:	

Website:	
Username:	
Password:	
Notes / Security Questions:	

Website:	
Username:	
Password:	
Notes / Security Questions:	

Website:	
Username:	
Password:	
Notes / Security Questions:	

Website:	
Username:	
Password:	
Notes / Security Questions:	

Website:	
Username:	
Password:	
Notes / Security Questions:	

Website:	
Username:	
Password:	
Notes / Security Questions:	

Website:	
Username:	
Password:	
Notes / Security Questions:	

Website:	
Username:	
Password:	
Notes / Security Questions:	

Website:	
Username:	
Password:	
Notes / Security Questions:	

Website:	
Username:	
Password:	
Notes / Security Questions:	

Website:	
Username:	
Password:	
Notes / Security Questions:	

Website:	
Username:	
Password:	
Notes / Security Questions:	

Website:	
Username:	
Password:	
Notes / Security Questions:	

Website:	
Username:	
Password:	
Notes / Security Questions:	

Website:	
Username:	
Password:	
Notes / Security Questions:	

Website:	
Username:	
Password:	
Notes / Security Questions:	

Website:	
Username:	
Password:	
Notes / Security Questions:	

Website:	
Username:	
Password:	
Notes / Security Questions:	

Website:	
Username:	
Password:	
Notes / Security Questions:	

Website:	
Username:	
Password:	
Notes / Security Questions:	

Website:	
Username:	
Password:	
Notes / Security Questions:	

Website:	
Username:	
Password:	
Notes / Security Questions:	

Website:	
Username:	
Password:	
Notes / Security Questions:	

Website:	
Username:	
Password:	
Notes / Security Questions:	

Website:	
Username:	
Password:	
Notes / Security Questions:	

Website:	
Username:	
Password:	
Notes / Security Questions:	

Website:	
Username:	
Password:	
Notes / Security Questions:	

Z

Website:	
Username:	
Password:	
Notes / Security Questions:	

Website:	
Username:	
Password:	
Notes / Security Questions:	

Website:	
Username:	
Password:	
Notes / Security Questions:	

Website:	
Username:	
Password:	
Notes / Security Questions:	

Website:	
Username:	
Password:	
Notes / Security Questions:	

Website:	
Username:	
Password:	
Notes / Security Questions:	

Website:	
Username:	
Password:	
Notes / Security Questions:	

Website:	
Username:	
Password:	
Notes / Security Questions:	

Z

Website:	
Username:	
Password:	
Notes / Security Questions:	

Website:	
Username:	
Password:	
Notes / Security Questions:	

Website:	
Username:	
Password:	
Notes / Security Questions:	

Website:	
Username:	
Password:	
Notes / Security Questions:	

Z

Website:	
Username:	
Password:	
Notes / Security Questions:	

Website:	
Username:	
Password:	
Notes / Security Questions:	

Website:	
Username:	
Password:	
Notes / Security Questions:	

Website:	
Username:	
Password:	
Notes / Security Questions:	

www.ingramcontent.com/pod-product-compliance
Lightning Source LLC
LaVergne TN
LVHW051744050326
832903LV00029B/2714